Butterfly in a Mason Jar

A Collection of Original Poems

By Brittany Brasher

This collection is dedicated to young Brashers who have yet to learn their powers. May you learn never to believe the world when they try to define and refine you.

Stand in your truth.
Always.

Captured

- Be My Valentine Baby
- You Know I'll Never Hurt You
- Senses Stroked
- Drunken Thoughts
- Silence
- Spoon

Cocooning

- Open Letter to All Who Will Listen
"The Heart of the Matter"
- Fading Innocence
- Desperado
- Powerful Acceptance [Learning Self-Love]
- Moving Out

Released into the Wild

- Jaggedly Remodeled
- Broken Beauty Breakthroughs
- Deadass
- Goddess Hidden Within
- I Wish I Was Healed
- Mahogany Man
- Tattoo

Captured: (verb)
take in one's possession or control by force.

Sometimes all we know is all that has consumed us. We make space for it to engulf us within it under the guise that we are living life. That is not the case. We allow ourselves to be captured by someone else's backstory of who we should be based on how we fit into the imaginings of their dreams. A milder version of Stockholm's Syndrome is surviving under the mindset that their dreams are yours - all the while ignoring the physical reminders that your intuition sends trying to let you know that you aren't supposed to be there at all.

Capturing a butterfly only benefits the person who holds the glass. The butterfly eventually learns to be captured and is taken out of its natural context which is to just exist - beautifully.

Be My Valentine, Baby

Roses are red,
Violets are bleu,
God blessed me
The day he sent you
Your charming smile
And warm embrace
Makes me want to kiss your face

Roses are red
Violets are bleu,
I can't wait
To spend my life with you
Marriage, kids, big beautiful house
We are sharing our dreams,
And planning them out.

Roses are red,
Violets are bleu.
I've given you my heart
It's past overdue.
Handle with care,
Like you always do
And I'll do the same
Because I love you.

Roses are red,
Violets are bleu.
You're my prince charming,
I'll be a princess for you.
Soon enough though,
we'll be King and Queen
Growing together
And living your dream.

You Know I'll Never Hurt You

"You know I'll never hurt you right?!"
You were my midnight escape. Late night chocolate express with a hint of vanilla
I distinctly remember running into your arms when I needed to be held.
Jones'n for the bones when I wanted to be loved.
In the same 5 seconds you promised not to hurt me, you inflicted more pain than I could ever know.
Before you, I was pure as ice - not that LA tap water ice, I'm talking Brita filter y'all!

Our silhouettes became one, skins collided, sheets absorbed our mixed prespirational scents, creating the perfect perfume; and we wore it all night
Even after you left me to bask in the essence of your glow...still waiting on my own.
Waking up in a stance of regrets, embraced by the cacophony you made as you quickly dressed and escaped
Taking the piece of me that cannot be replaced
Exchanging my adolescence for womanhood with every breathtaking thrust
Staining my sheets and rearranging the alphabet to sound like a name that wasn't mine
You came, and went.
"WE AIN'T LOVIN' GIRL, WE JUST FUCKIN!"
Slowly, your "I owe you's" turned into "I love you's" as you lost yourself in our rush for animalistic passion and I finally decided not to keep up.
You loved me, you lost me, and now you can't find me
Because we were just fuckin in the first place.

Senses Stroked

I can imagine your touch.
Something I have never felt before,
Stroking the soulful parts of my being
Allowing me to access parts of myself that I had tucked away;
Tightly wrapped up and hidden.

I can feel your kiss on my lips.
So light and kind,
Caressing my mind as the thoughts dance with an
eloquent rage that can only be attached to the idea of pleasure
In the making.

I can see you reaching for me.
Back turned to the sun,
Facing the giant prince that you have become
in the fairy tales I created in my imagination.

I embrace you.
Becoming everything I have been asking for
Without me saying a word;
Knowing when to show up and when to give space,
Understanding the subtleness that is needed for the creativity to
flow and love to be shared.

I can sense the love between us.
The possibility of it growing,
The reassuring moments of clarity that are created when the
space is shared between us
Understanding that you spark thoughts that never had space
before
Pushing me to trust myself more
Connect with the Divine within
You never even know what you do for me
To me,

with me.

In my mind,
We are free,
Young,
Wild,
Together.
In love
With ourselves and each other.
I am safe here.
Sensing you all around me,
Enveloping me in love, light and the liberties that come with
confident thoughts,
Sensible actions,
Emotional balance,
Lust and love all at the same time-
For you and me

I am finding myself, trying to find you.
While you are letting me find myself
Waiting for me to arrive at what you already can see
Beauty,
Brilliance,
Belonging.

I sense you.
All around.
I'm growing toward the light that you provide
the sunflower's myth;
Turning to each other to accept and support one another
There is nothing else for me but than here
For now
At least.

Drunken Thoughts

I wonder why they call it liquid courage?
Probably because
These words have been trapped in a never ending escapade
Inside the vault stored at the bottom of my heart
Sealed with the front of my mind

Frontal being
Picked by these gasses
That create such a sweet aroma
And dangerous combination when
Mixed with sodas.
I drown out the pain of loss,
Hurt,
Anger, as I
Sip,
Sip,
Sip,
'Til my physical is in danger
Of being lost in the shuffle,
Caught in the scuffle
Of adventure.
Blacked out.

I
Hit the ground running every time
"Why you always hungover?!
Drinking the night before an important day?!"
You can catch me, Bree
Hanging out the car door,
As I expel my insides,
Coughing up the night before
In some
Yellow glob of bile.
Heaving,

Coughing,
Wishing,
I
Didn't take that last shot.
Hoping that I can feel better by 5 o'clock,
'Cause a bitch can't bounce back like she used to!

Red flags I turned to blue;
Things I ignored because I wanted you.

I can see clearly now the rain is gone.
Hindsight is 20/20 and my glasses just
Stopped being blurry.
I
Wiped off with fogged breath
Smudged fingerprints,
Facial oils and
Lash strides dipped in tears from the years wasted

I'm back!!
Alive and better than ever
What we doin' this weekend?
Because the turn up is real!
I'll never forget the feel
Of how you used to hold me at night.
Grab me and squeeze me
So tight, i forget to breathe
And then with ease
I let go.

Let you see that life without me was just a tease
So now, you calling me at 4 am.
The tables have turned
I hope you learned
That I just
Wanted you safe.

In my arms, or that of another.
Alive.
Breathing.
Thriving.
Succeeding.
Living your best life!
With
Or without
Me.

I wanted to see the king you became
Even if I didn't have a claim.
I would have watched the throne,
In awe
Of the royal nature and majestic stature.

I saw your potential,
Fell for it,
Expected nothing less,
And was robbed of the very thing.

You sent me higher.
But I got paranoid
And now I avoid you at all costs.
Except for Sundays.
When I steal glances of you
Through side eyes and "look at your neighbors and say.."

You were my world once
And now I drown you in the fire;
Purifying your image,
Asking my crystal ball
If the decision was the right one.
Waiting for an answer,
Knowing
I would never have asked these questions

Had I not taken that last shot
And now,
Here it comes,
Passing through my body
Uncontrollably,
Watch out!

Will you still love me tomorrow?

Silence

Sometimes it feels like silence is the only option.
Like that's the only way you know I exist;
Like finding me in my secluded state is the perfect karma for your
torment.

Sometimes I tremble at the power of my own voice.
Like I don't trust the words to form fully;
Like I don't believe I have the power to make my message clear to
you.

Sometimes I am afraid I am wrong.
Like I am living in an alternate reality;
Like everything I do needs to be overthought to the point of ex-
haustion.

Sometimes I wonder if I am enough.
Like the pain inside is all I have,
Like the wounds won't properly heal and no one will love me past
them.

Sometimes I wish I wasn't me.
Like there is someone better to be;
Like someone else out there has their shit figured out past this
point.

Sometimes I lay awake and cry.
Like you aren't laying by my side;
Like you can't hear me silently sobbing myself to sleep;
In darkness.

Sometimes I wish you'd care;
Like the guys in the movies;
Like there is a thought that exists outside of what is good for you,
alone.

Sometimes I wonder, why me?
Like this isn't the destiny I chose;
Like this isn't the life I was supposed to live; with all these curve-balls

Sometimes it feels so cold.
Like no one will understand;
Like the complexities of my questions will never be answered by any-one

Sometimes it feels like silence is the only option.
Like I would burden you with my thoughts;
Like I overthought all these feelings and cannot trust my instincts anymore.

Sometimes is happening more than usual.
Like I am losing track of time;
Like everything is on an endless loop and I have yet to choose the correct response to release me.

Spoon

Collecting
The deposits.
I became,
Stuck
In the corners.

You scooped me up.
Before I am
Left,
Dissolving
In the wetness of despair.

Lifting me out of the cold,
Lonely places I have been;
Adding me
To the rest of the
Collected deposits;
Left
Over.

Cocooning: (verb)
envelope or surround in a protective or comforting way

Separation in itself is a version of cocooning. Going into self and understanding what you need, taking stock of what is and adjusting to realize everything that you wish for yourself is necessary and a remedy to being captured. Seeming herder on the exterior in order to let the softeners bake and perfect before the next phase is actualized.

An Open Letter to All Who Will Listen
"The Heart of the Matter"

I forgive you...
> For making me feel unwanted.
> For forcing me to find my beauty in the eyes of many unworthy men.
> For not being around to wipe my tears and whisk me away from the darkness.
> For unintentionally sewing my heart on my sleeve, making my vulnerabilities known and not staying around long enough to protect me from the world.
> For not being my example to follow and search for.
> For betraying my innocent trust with your broken promises and empty conversations.

You never know the detriment your presence has on someone until it's no longer felt. I missed the void you left and try to fill it every chance I get. Clinging to the first man I deem worthy of my time captured with just a simple glance or compliment. It's funny because they seem to be a lot like you in some way. I know that love is a two way street and so I must be absolved of my painful ways as well...

So, forgive me...
> For ever making you feel as if you weren't enough.
> For not reaching out sooner.
> For not saying "I love you" more.
> For asking myself "How could a man be so dumb to make the same mistake three times?"
> For envying these young girls when they rattle off facts about their fathers that existed in their imaginations and realities alike, as I stand, stone-faced, lock-jawed and silent; hurting because I could not do the same.

Forgive me for standing here, at 22 and allowing my pride to translate
what I really want to say is...

Because you weren't here,
    I find you in other places,
    Molded in other men's faces.

I've subsided the pain and let the pleasure pour through.

Because you weren't here,
    I am drawn to strong arms and ears being lent,
    Hearts that mean good but words that suggest otherwise.

Because you weren't here,
    I find LOVE in LUSTFUL interactions.
    I am scared to trust my gut,
    Quick to give benefits of the doubt and slow to walk away -
    I'd rather be pushed.

But yet, here I stand; at 22, understanding you're the missing
piece.
    The catalyst that set this whole dynamic in motion.

Here I am,
    Understanding that I am capable of greatness and you are a
    prime benefactor of my success.
    Trust issues, hurt and a sharp tongue;
    All symbols of this daddy-less daddy's girl.

Thank you.
    For pushing me to be the strong, independent, black woman I
    am today.

Bold. Bald-headed. Beautifully yours.

Fading Innocence

Ladybugs don't bring good luck,
Dreams don't come true,
Everything I thought you were - you turned out to be!

How could something so small change the world?

I still hurt when I hear your name.
I see your face and my heart breaks all over again.
Any word sparks a memory so intricate, I let go of myself
just to spend a little more time with you.
Breathing in your essence,
Staring into the abyss your eyes represent.

I stopped believing dreams come true.

You were my midnight escape.
The rendezvous that raced through my mind when my
eyelids stopped telling time.
You never crossed over to the light,
You stayed in the shadows of my memory,
Reality is nothing but a reminder of what I can't have.

You were everything I thought you'd be!

A lying, cheating, no good son of a woman who must not
realize just how much you lack.
You left me probing my mind,
Trying to figure out what I did to push you so far from me.
Every now and then, a little piece of me wishes I wouldsa
gave you some of me.
So I won't feel so dumb when I wake up - alone.
Disoriented - not understanding why and when you snuck
away from me so quickly
Out the trap door that brought you here.

That would make the lies a little more bearable.
At least I would have gotten a little more out of this mutual
excuse for "time well spent" than a wastebasket full of regrets,
     A pillow - soggy from the crocodile tears that didn't bring you
     back to me,
     And the black hole that plagues the next soul to come along.

Desperado

I am not disappointed,
I am lonely.

I feel like all I have to offer is sex.
And he took it,
Without a doubt.

And now,
I am all that I have left;
With no one to share myself with.

This sucks.
When will I learn?

Powerful Acceptance [Learning Self Love]

I am falling in love with the skin I am in,
Mesmerized by the way my thighs meet,
Dazed as the sun kisses my skin,
Creating this timeless glow.
Understanding the shape of my hips
Speak volumes.
As I walk with pride
Loudly proclaiming over the insecurity of my
Midsection;
I am the shit!
Real talk.

Self love never had a section in the books I buried myself in.
Hiding from reality in the pages of someone else's experience,
Making my brain the centerpiece of my existence,
Being noticed for my beauty.
Being talked out of spaces.
"You should be a model" became the biggest insult anyone could say aloud.
As i was dismissed from being educated,
Thrown into the wasteland of beautiful faces that I would never measure up to.

To consider your beauty in a world that bashes it is a revolutionary act.
Well,
I did always want to be a rebel.
In search, i'm finding:
There is no petition to sign validating beauty in blackness.
There is no protest to attend uplifting cellulite on skin.
There is no group that meets to plan an attack on dispelling black woman's masculinity.
I can only be one of two black women in America:
An empowered male bashing afro-centric educator;

Or
A spectator to my identity, baptized in the river of Eurocentric
beliefs and beauty standards - dying to my true self every day

But what about the grey area?
The parts that people don't speak about?
The womanhood that personifies love?
That's my womanhood,
That's my beauty,
That's my superpower.

Love of self permits the love of a nation,
And I have the power to build just that.
All in the switch of a hip,
The batting of an eye,
A conversation on the subjugation of the African American male and
involuntary invisibleness of the African American woman.
I am and can be a Multifaceted Goddess;
Speaking life, healing and love into everyone I meet,
Moving mountains by simply planting my feet.
So deep into the earth
The world rotates differently.

Woman is life
Life is
me.

Moving Out

My heart desires something greater than what I've been getting
here.
Something more inclusive and holistic than the love you force feed
me.
Submission comes naturally and I've fought you tooth and nail, every step of the way.

Sacrificing myself and goals to HELP you reach yours,
Losing sight of my passions and desires
Beneath the clout that your process takes.

I've birthed your visions like the children I am supposed to yearn
for.
Thriving as a single mother,
Loving broken boys to men unworthy of the goddess I am.
Unlearning ways to love myself in order to expand and enhance your
level of comfort in your manhood.
WHAT TYPE OF SHIT IS THAT?!

How does my womanhood emasculate you so much?
"I wouldn't want you if you let someone else fuck you!"
How dare you point a crooked finger in my direction when you are the
reason I have been deflowered and dethroned?!

My past is painted in smudged charcoal because of its handlers, not
because of I.

I,
who have so gracefully attempted to protect me innocence and royal
nature.
I,
who have so independently built the foundation of self from pure
love.
I,

who have suffered and regrouped around the jagged edges left by lovers unworthy to watch the throne.

Consider this the 30-day.
No need to scramble to regroup or get shit together.
As I stared into your eyes, I noticed something different today.

Me.
The me that deserves the love I give returned.
The me that deserves to be paid attention to.
The me that needs a partner that won't ask for an instructional manual before interacting with me.
The me that I have slept on for so many years.
The me that is standing strong enough to say that I have to walk away.

For me,
The move out is just the beginning of standing up for me.

Released into the wild:

Release: (verb)
allow or enable to escape from confinement; to set free

Wild: (noun)
living or growing in the natural environment

When you open your eyes to the reality that surrounds you, it may
be a situation where you feel that you have been captured when
in reality you have been allowing yourself to be contained or even con-
taining yourself in the hopes of pleasing others. This disconnection
from your natural state and environment creates distance and helps
aid in the process of losing yourself. When you get to a point where
you decide to step out of your own way and lose yourself in the pro-
cess of naturally living in your skin, you have done it. You have given
yourself permission to live out loud and set yourself free!

Jaggedly Remodeled

How am I supposed to contain myself?
Who puts me back together this time?
Who catched the string attached to my sanity as it begins to float
toward the sun?

I do.
No one else is brave enough to touch the jagged pieces
Left behind from the movements that persisted through the
years.

I do.
Because when no one was looking,
The young girl inside
Grew
Stronger with every tear shed.

I do.
Who else will know where all the pieces go?
Who else will understand the beautiful complexity that exists when
you have to adjust
And recreate a masterpiece?
Young goddess,
You were never supposed to be contained.
Spread your wings,
Share your gift,
Touch the world and change it.

Beautiful dream child,
No one deserves the power to put you together.
You aren't broken,
You're simply mid-shift and confused.
Trust you intuition,
Root yourself in your ability to morph,
Step into your greatness.

Lovely creature,
Sanity is subjective.
Not one person has completely captured its entirety.
You may be the first.
Trust the sun, as it will rise again;
Shining through your jaggedness like stained glass art
Highlighting your radiant essence,
Kissing the skin you are in,
Despite the topsy turvy whirlwind that you feel caught in.

Hurt doesn't break you;
It separates you from your comfort zone,
      Just long enough for you to look up and see yourself some
      where different,
Gives you time to change the course of your life through healing,
Makes space for you to breathe and hear your thoughts as they
loudly proclaim your greatness.

You are not broken.
You are a masterpiece.
You are worthy of love.
You are not alone.
You are carrying a world on your shoulders so gracefully,
      No one notices the pain but you.
You give purpose to the steps you take,
      not that they haven't been taken before.

Broken Beauty Breakthroughs

I tried to see my beauty through the eyes of others.
I got let down every time.
Their vision blurred the lines of my soul,
Etched my spirited sense of self with overindulgence.
They tried to erase the parts they couldn't make excuses for.
They made excuses for the parts they studied to understand.

I gave my power away to the audience I had created.
Let them define who and what I would become
Their imaginations could not hold the essence that I possess.
I over achieved in their world and failed in my own.
They pushed me to be proud and yet I still feel ungrown.
They celebrated my triumphs while I sulked in self pity.

I sold my happiness to the highest bidder.
Cloaked in the duty that rested on my shoulders.
The unmistakable feeling that I needed to save my bloodline,
I auctioned off what I knew to be true in exchange for someone
else's dreams.
They never asked what dreams I held for my own future.
They never pushed me outside of my comfort zone.

I made due with what I had.
I survived melancholy lifestyles.
I rooted myself in the planter's pot,
Growing slowly but striving for more
They did not transplant me.
They let me rot and smiled the whole time.

I blame myself for what is happening.
How could I not fight harder?
Surviving was never the plan, thriving is what I was made to do
Who and what I am is what I decide.
They can take it, or
They can leave it

Deadass

Why did you look at me that way if you didn't intend on keeping me?
Why did you love me all day if you only planned to leave me...
Guessing,
Wondering,
Overthinking,
Asking what this could be at every moment.

Second guessing,
Rewinding memories,
Reminiscing,

Deadass.
I hate that I gave you so much space,
So much priority,
So much of my energy
'Cause deadass...
I want you.
For more than just a vacation escapade
Your energy persists beyond the distance of the seas and yet I still feel like your unavailable.

I want to be heartless, but my surveillance of the facts have me thinking otherwise.

You showed me what I wanted and couldn't find the words to ask for.
You made me feel seen and understood while being silent.

Settled to tears,
I'm not this person.
Too close to walk away,
Too far to forget,
Too attached to not be bothered,
Too bothered to not be attached.

Deadass

I like you.
I liked you before you made me feel stupid for liking you.
Before you included me in the indiscretion that I involved myself in
before your transparency was a thing.

Now, with tear stained cheeks and blurry vision
More than my glasses will allow
I bid you good day young man!
For only a young man can awaken the love in a woman with no inten-
tion or expectation
Without knowing exactly what he wants

Deadass.

What the fuck was I thinking?!
How the fuck did I fall so hard, so fast?!
I'd love to blame it on you and say that you made it easy
I wouldn't be lying at all, but...
I didn't make it hard.

Who let the guards off so early the night you stroked my skin and
touched my soul with your strong and gentle caress.

Deadass.
That shit was life.

The Goddess Hidden Within

I've been
Manifesting my destiny since I could remember
There were no coincidences only positive thoughts that triggered
Life events
Took their toll
I grew, strong
Brash
And bold.

Planted. When I thought I was stuck
Watered. When I thought I cried too much.
These
Goddess vibes were endowed on a real one

Everybody wanna piece
But they can't control
All these positive vibes buried within my soul
So deep,
It surprises me even.
When I speak,
I change the seasons.
Depression doesn't live here when I'm at my peak.

They choke on my aura,
Surpassing that
Lump of pride in their throat,
They panic.
Off top.

I watch.
In awe.
As they spit out everything they think I've done to them.
Every wrong choice I made with them in mind,
Blaming me for all the insecurities they possess

All the pain in their chest as they struggle to digest
What may have been the best damned thing to happen to them
quite frankly.

When in reality, they were never capable of holding on to such a pow-
erful woman.

Worthy adversary of an egotistical man.
Thinking to myself...
Well damn!

Some turn green,
Others turn blue,
Most turn the backs,
Unsure of what to do.

I figure they embarrassed themselves
Because I'm fucking awesome.
There is no way in the world that this was all me.

Was I too honest?
Too independent?
That's me.

I'd rather depend on myself than be disappointed by your lack of
follow through, consistency and understanding of self.

I refuse to continuously water myself down so that you can have an
easier swallow.
Fuck that!
When you stepped to me
You should have done your research.
You would have seen
That i was more that a cute face and slim waist
I am woman

I am life
Im not your momma or wife.

I am made in the image of god, she
Molded me in Aphrodite's delicate form.
I've been kissed by Sun Ra himself.

So don't call me shorty,
Don't call me Mami,
Call me by my name.

Brittany Marie Brasher

I am woman
and I refuse to take the blame
For any reason that you feel inadequate.

It is not my job to raise you,
Nurturing past your flaws,
While neglecting my own happiness,
Loving you more than me.
"Well sometimes that's how it be"
I refuse to accept this as reality.

So do me a favor,
Step outside of your comfort zone,
Hike the mountains of fear,
Campout with your subconscious,
Heal your hurt before you include me in your Journey

I Wish I Was Healed

I am tired of watching you prick your fingers
On the broken pieces, you insist on picking up.

You shouldn't have to clean up the mess these other "men" made...
...and yet - you continue to stay

I deserve you and you deserve me.
I love you and you feel the same.
I abuse you and you...just take the pain
Knowing the greatness of my potential.

I hate that and yet I am honored to be receiving your unconditional
love

I don't want it to change.
Let's make this permanent.

Affectionately yours,

Broken-hearted,
Under-taker,
over-lover.

Mahogany Man

The sun frames you as you slumber,
Creating an effortless glow that serenades me as I watch your
dreams flash across your face.
You are a sleeping beauty.
A naturally, man-made force to be reckoned with.

Your Mahogany spreads so delicately over every inch of your being,
Seeping into parts deeper than others,
Creating such a unique pattern of postulated freckles and moles
Perfectly placed, so that nature itself mimics your form.
Perfect.
Skin,
Only split by pearls of white when you share your happiness with
me
Cheeks meeting windows to your soul,
As you gush in laughter and joy,
Pinching the edges of eyes closed,
Eyelashes greeting each other with such a sweet surrender.

Mahogany man, you are mesmerizing.
I creep to observe such a creature as you.
With so much love,
I watch you do what you do.
Day in,
Day out,
Making space for the grace you embed in your very waltz on this
earth.

You looked
So...
Peaceful
In your sleep.
Lips pursed ever so slightly.
Face resting,

Made my heart skip beats.
The only thing better than seeing you in this state,
Is watching you wake up and smile at me, again.
It is then,
At that point,
That I fully understand
What is is to be of this world;
Your world.
Mahogany man.

Tattoo

I have
Pierced my skin multiple times.
Each time
Bracing the physical pain effortlessly
In an attempt to hide my appearance even from myself.
Chastising myself with a physical reminder of an emotional weakness
Showcased for the world to see.

I've burned my body
Etching ink in it.
Each time forming a pattern
Often seen clearer once zoomed out.
Carving out moons and suns into my planetary existence
My shell, hollowing out as a reminder to remain steadfast and true
to self.

I've plucked, raked, and braided my scalp on countless occasions.
Each time, undoing its natural order
Bending my kinks and coils backward
Until snapping was the only option.
Irreversible damage by heat and hands
Until I became someone else.

I've learned to adjust to the chaos around me.
So much so, that it's hard to distinguish myself from it.
Drowning my true self and honest intentions,
Ignoring my needs and my humanity each time,
Pushing and pulling at my essence as a way to create inner comfort
For an outer world.
That is not purely my own, to begin with
I have been...
Broken,
In many ways over the years.
Emotionally flawed.

Mentally impaired.
Physically bruised and battered.
Blood rushing to the top of skin,
Exposing my sensitive nature.
Bubbling up and swelling in the sun,
Blistering and spilling over as blood runs, adjacent to my pumping
heart.
I have had flesh ripped open,
emotions ignored,
silenced.
beat me near to death;

And honestly,
I am left alone
Rushed to heal, one scab at a time.

I have been healing from this reality.
Plagued with violent reminders of my identity.
Ignorant to my needs,
Absolved of any responsibilities for actions against me,
I am finally able to see
This world was not made for me.
Rather, I am a byproduct of a simple mistake
Made time and time again until it becomes habit.
Errors sending the strongest
Into a space of despair.
"Inaccuracy" reads the barcode that riddles my bones.
I am always sold with a warning label,
Caution tape is what holds me together.

Each piercing, burning, priming desire I hold,
Will always lead you to fools gold.
Pity the fool who find value in my existence;
A soul never wanting to rest in a world never meant for it.
Comfort in chaos is an oasis.
An activist at heart will never let their guard down,

Seeking conundrums at every twist and turn
Surrounded by a world that would never see
Past the chaos
I so eloquently hide in.
I will continue to heal
No matter what is done to me.

www.ingramcontent.com/pod-product-compliance
Lightning Source LLC
Chambersburg PA
CBHW060357130626
46553CB00003B/1270